DRUGS AND YOUR BROTHERS AND SISTERS

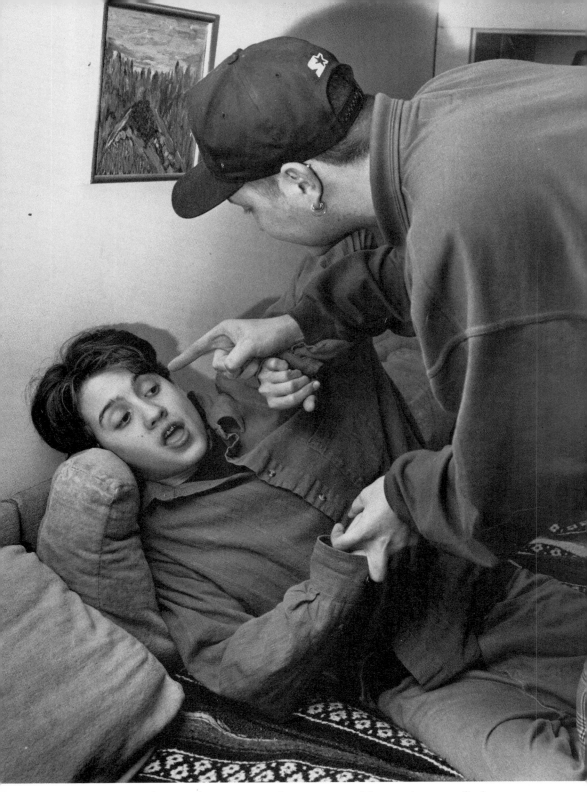

Brothers and sisters sometimes come to blows when one finds
out that the other is into drugs.

THE DRUG ABUSE PREVENTION LIBRARY

DRUGS AND YOUR BROTHERS AND SISTERS

Rhoda McFarland

THE ROSEN PUBLISHING GROUP, INC.

NEW YORK

Published in 1992, 1993, 1997 by The Rosen Publishing Group, Inc.
29 East 21st Street, New York, NY 10010

Revised Edition 1997

Copyright © 1992, 1993, 1997 by The Rosen Publishing Group, Inc.

Library of Congress Cataloging-in-Publication Data

McFarland, Rhoda.
  Drugs and your brothers and sisters/by Rhoda McFarland.
  (The Drug Abuse Prevention Library)
  Includes bibliographical references and index.
  Summary: Discusses the effect of drug abuse on the family, particularly siblings, of the abuser and what family members can do to help each other.
    ISBN 0-8239-2582-X
    1. Teenagers—United States—Drug abuse—Juvenile literature.   2. Narcotic addicts—United States—Family relationships—Juvenile literature. 3. Drug abuse—United States—Prevention—Juvenile literature.   4. Brothers and sisters—United States—Juvenile literature.   [1. Drug abuse. 2. Family problems.   3. Brothers and sisters.] I. Title.   II. Series.
    HV5824.Y68M39   1997
    362.29′132—dc20   90-49277
                                                CIP
                                                AC

Manufactured in the United States of America

Contents

Introduction

When Michelle came in, Brandon glared at her and left the room. He hadn't spoken to her in a week and wanted nothing to do with her. Everyone knew she was using drugs. Even worse, she was having sex with anybody and everybody. He was disgusted and embarrassed to be her brother. She lived in the same house, but he didn't have to talk to her or be around her.

Brandon's anger toward his sister is a natural reaction to her behavior. She is causing him pain. Drug users don't just hurt themselves; they affect everyone around them. Those people closest to them are most affected.

Addiction isn't just the addict's problem.
It's a family problem.

This book explains the changes that drug use causes the user and his or her family. It looks at the problem from the viewpoint of the brother or sister of a drug user and explains how behavior changes as teens go from experimenting to full addiction.

Parents also change as their teens progress through the stages of dependence. The book contains information to help you understand what happens to you as your parents and the drug user change.

After you know what is going on, you can look at ways to help. This book offers suggestions on how to help the user, your parents, and yourself.

An early sign of growing drug involvement is loss of pride in your appearance.

CHAPTER 1

My Brother Is a Drug Addict

Lincoln School Library

*R*obin stood looking out the window as the police car drove away with her brother. The thoughts raced around in her head. *That's my brother Mark being taken to the police station in handcuffs. It was bad enough when he got caught shoplifting. At least no one else knew about it. This is awful. The whole neighborhood watched the cops take him away. He was caught robbing houses with his druggie friends. They did anything to get money for drugs. He must be out of his mind to hang out with them. They're . . . oh, God, they're all drug addicts, and Mark is too. My brother is a drug addict.*

10 | *Drug Addiction*

Robin wonders if Mark is out of his mind. In a way, he is. Because of his drug use, Mark's mind isn't working right. His drug use is not just a bad habit. He has a disease—a disease called chemical dependence.

Like any other disease, chemical dependence has symptoms. When Mark first started drinking, he got buzzed on a couple of beers. Now, he needs a six-pack to get that same feeling. Needing more of a drug to get the same feeling is called tolerance. It is a symptom of growing dependence. Mark also says he doesn't have a problem. His denial, or unwillingness to admit the truth, is another symptom of his disease.

If Mark stops using drugs, he may break out in a sweat and feel sick to his stomach. Those are signs of physiological dependence on drugs. His body needs them. Constantly thinking about using, and feeling that you need the drug to get through the day (or a specific situation), is psychological dependence.

Once Mark starts using, he doesn't know when he will stop. Addiction is the uncontrollable compulsion to use a drug and to continue using no matter what happens.

Chemical dependence is a progressive disease. That is, it gets worse the longer someone uses the drug. The only way to end the progression is to stop using the drug.

Even if Mark stops using, he will still be chemically dependent. Chemical dependence cannot be cured. However, it can be controlled, as long as a person doesn't use the drug anymore.

High Risks for Addiction

Children of alcoholics and drug users are most at risk for addiction. Research shows that alcoholism can run in families. If you have a blood relative who is an alcoholic, your chance of becoming chemically dependent is very high. Siblings of drug users are also more at risk.

Are You Addicted?

If you drink or use other drugs, you may have a problem and not know it. It doesn't matter how much, or how often, you drink or use drugs. It's what happens to you when you use them. Ask yourself the following questions. If you answer yes to any of them, you may be in trouble with chemicals.

- Do your friends have to tell you what you did because you don't remember? This is called a blackout. It is a very serious warning sign that you are in trouble with chemicals.
- Do you say you will not get drunk and then do it anyway?
- Have you ever felt sick while using but kept on using?
- Do you gulp down the first few drinks?
- Do you want an extra hit to get you going?
- Have your friends said you are drinking or using other drugs too much?
- Do you think about drinking or using?
- Do you talk a lot about partying?
- Have your grades been going down?
- Are you having more problems with your parents?
- Have you ever felt guilty about something you did when you were high?
- Do you lie about how much you use?
- Do you drink or use other drugs to forget your problems?
- Do you drink or use other drugs alone?
- Do you get into fights when you drink or use?

CHAPTER 2

Why Teens Start Using Drugs

Shaking his head, Jerry closed the door to his room. Pam is really blowing it, he thought. She doesn't listen to anybody. She used to listen to me even when she wouldn't listen to Mom and Dad. Now she tells me to buzz off. Partying is all she thinks about. Why did she start doing drugs? She knows better.

What Causes Drug Use?

Teens begin drinking and using other drugs for many reasons. When someone brought beer to a party one night, Pam drank with everyone else. She knew she shouldn't. Her parents would not like it. But doing something forbidden felt exciting.

A warning signal of drug or alcohol dependence is loss of interest in your room or prized possessions.

Most teens say that they think their friends won't like them if they don't join in doing drugs. Peer pressure is hard to resist.

By hanging out with drug users, teens often find a group that accepts them, as well as a chemical that makes them feel good. It seems to be the answer to their problems.

Many times you feel very unsure of yourself. You may feel hopeless, and think you can't do anything right. At times you may feel that no one likes you. When all of these feelings come together, you feel very depressed. That is when some teens use alcohol and other drugs to feel better.

Many teens are like Robin's brother, Mark. Mark's parents pressure him to go to college and "make something" of himself. They push Mark to do better. Mark feels that he is never good enough. He worries about failing. His fear is so great that on test days he feels sick. When Mark gets high on marijuana, he doesn't have those terrible feelings.

Michelle's terrible feelings come from being so shy. She is sure that anything she says will be stupid. She feels that no one wants to be around her. She wishes she could be like other kids.

16 | Michelle has found that when she drinks, she loses those awful feelings of shyness. She can talk to people without being afraid. Alcohol helps her feel socially acceptable.

Some teens hear about getting high and wonder what it's like. They start using just because they are curious. Before they know it, they are hooked.

People also get started on drugs after watching their parents. When Mike was small, his father gave him sips of his beer. When Mike was twelve, he and his father drank beer and watched the ball game together on television. By then, Mike knew where his father kept a stash of marijuana. Mike helped himself to that when nobody was around.

Parents don't have to drink with their children to give the message that it is okay. Parents who use drugs set an example that the way to deal with life is to use drugs. Remember, addiction can run in families. The social patterns in the family that support the dependence are very strong.

Why do people start using alcohol or another drug? It changes the way they feel. It helps them forget their problems. But it also makes those problems worse

Hiding a joint is just one of the sneaky habits teens fall into when they start to abuse drugs.

18 | and causes people more problems. As problems get worse, users no longer feel good using the drugs. They must use more to feel not as bad.

What makes drug use so appealing? The society you live in is a drug-using, pleasure-seeking society. You feel pressure to use drugs. Once the drug use starts, you don't know where it will go.

What started for Pam as an exciting adventure could turn into the nightmare of addiction.

CHAPTER 3

The Addiction Process

Staring out of the car window, Sheryl thought of her brother Wes. Sheryl and her parents were on their way to see him. Wes was in a treatment center for alcoholism and drug addiction. How could that be? It seemed like just yesterday that Wes was laughing and giving Sheryl advice about boys. Suddenly, Wes wasn't laughing anymore. He was yelling and calling Sheryl names. What happened?

The changes in Wes were not sudden. Wes's disease progressed over time and through many stages. There were signs that he was getting into trouble.

20 | ## Stage 1: Experimenting

From the time Wes was little, his father gave him sips of beer. When he was in sixth grade, he and his friends sneaked beer out of their homes. They drank it behind bushes in the park. All of them felt a little buzz. It was exciting because they knew they were not supposed to do it. Wes liked to feel high. He brought two cans most of the time.

When school started, he met lots of new kids. One of them asked him if he wanted to smoke marijuana. Wanting to be part of the group, Wes said yes. The marijuana made him feel even better than beer did. He wanted to do it again.

Stage 2: Regular Use

Wes began going to parties regularly. It took four or five beers before Wes had a good buzz. He was developing a tolerance. He didn't like the hangovers, but so what? He liked to party. He could drink a lot and still feel okay. He bragged about it and called others "lightweights." Sometimes Wes had blackouts—he didn't remember what had happened the night before.

Wes lied about where he was going and what he was doing. He had to be careful

For the user, his supply is as near as the nearest phone—as long as he has the cash to pay for it.

22 where he put his stash. He didn't want anyone to find it. He was always short of money, so he took money from his mother's purse. He started dealing drugs to pay for his own drugs.

Wes had trouble getting home on time, so his parents were always grounding him for being late. Sometimes Wes stayed out all night. His parents got really upset then. He told them he had stayed at a friend's house. He said he had not called home because he didn't want to wake them. Lying was becoming a way of life for Wes.

Wes cut class sometimes and went to a friend's house to drink beer or get high. He missed wrestling practice because he forgot, or wanted to get high instead. Finally the coach cut him from the team. Wes said he didn't care.

When old friends tried to talk to Wes about what was happening, he got mad. He told them to buzz off. Thinking about getting high was all he cared about. Wes was entering the next stage.

Stage 3: Harmful Involvement
While Wes was not yet chemically dependent, he was harmfully involved with drugs. Alcohol and marijuana were not

enough. He tried anything that was around. He liked speed a lot. Acid and PCP were okay, but he didn't go looking for them. When he had the money, cocaine was his favorite.

By now, Wes was only interested in getting high. If he went to class, he was thrown out more often than not.

Home was a war zone. Wes's parents tried everything to make him shape up. It did no good. He got mad and took off for days. His sister, Sheryl, was such a goody-goody that Wes couldn't stand her. His little brother, Tommy, was all right. When the door was locked, Tommy always opened his bedroom window for Wes.

Wes stole the family silver and sold it for drugs. He let his friends in to steal the VCR. Anything of value disappeared from the house. There still wasn't enough money for the drugs Wes needed. His tolerance was so great that it took a lot to make him high. He began shoplifting with some of his friends. They got caught, but he didn't have to go to jail. It was his first time, so he was given a court date and sent home with his parents.

Wes's parents know that he does drugs. He doesn't care anymore. He told them there was nothing they could do about it.

The violence that often comes with drug use may cause siblings to fear for their lives.

What he didn't tell them was that there is *25*
nothing *he* can do about it, either. Wes is
addicted. He doesn't like what is happening to him, but he doesn't know how to
stop it.

Stage 4: Chemical Dependence

At this point addicts don't use drugs to
feel good. They use drugs to feel less bad.
Many parents give up. The only friends
addicts have are their drug-using buddies.
They are often physically ill. They get flu
and colds easily. They have no choice over
their using.

Addicts don't see that their drug use
is causing them problems. They blame
others for what is happening to them.
Even if they question their use, their need
is so great that they can't stop. They hate
themselves and often think about suicide.
They may want help, but many don't
know how to get it. Some are lucky and
ask for help or have people who get them
help. The unlucky ones die of their
addiction.

The time it takes to go from Stage 1 to
the end of Stage 3 is different for each
person. In some teens, the progression is
as fast as six months. Others might use
for a year before getting into real trouble.

26 | Teens who use cocaine can get to stage 4 within a couple of months. With crack cocaine, the addiction develops in a few weeks.

As the disease progresses in the teen, the family reacts to the unusual behavior. Family members develop their own form of the disease. This is the subject of the next two chapters.

CHAPTER 4

What Happens to Parents?

Staring at the blank paper, Lisa could not think of how to start her English assignment. All she could think about was how her parents were acting. What is wrong with them anyway? she thought. They have to know Rob is doing drugs. Why don't they do something about it? Mom is either crying or yelling. Dad calls Rob names and tells him to get out. Mom cries when Rob leaves, and Dad yells at her for babying Rob. Then they fight with each other. If I'm around they both yell at me. This place is a zoo.

Codependent Parents

The whole family is affected by a chemically dependent person. People affected

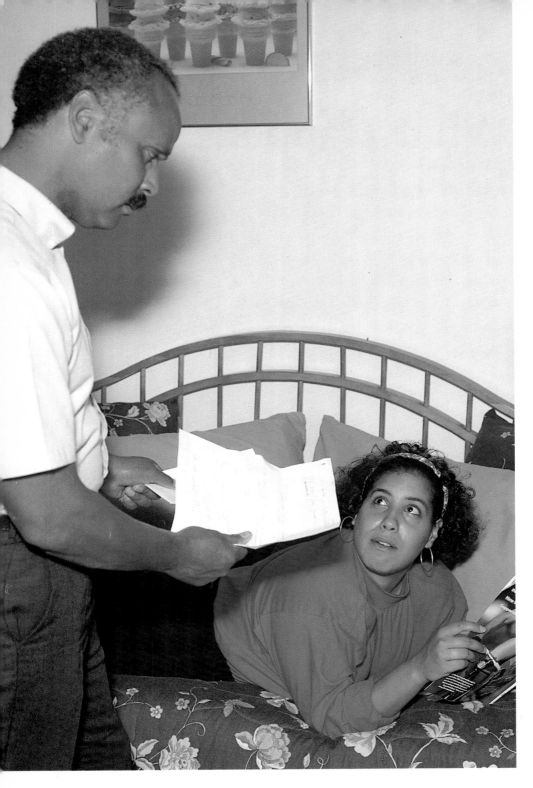

Falling grades and frequent truancy bring about angry family scenes.

by someone else's dependence are called codependent. Codependents behave strangely themselves. Parents of drug users may react to that added stress by acting unreasonable and confusing. Their behavior gets more unpredictable as their teen gets further into addiction.

Experimenting and Regular Use

During experimenting, not enough chemicals are used to change the teen's behavior. Parents don't notice any unusual behavior that makes them react.

In the early stages of regular use, problems start to come up at school. Rob's mother, Pat, got calls from teachers about his behavior in class. The attendance office called about his cutting class. Rob's mother said she would talk to him.

When teachers sent home notices of Rob's poor work, Rob made it sound as if they picked on him. Rob's father, Jim, went to school and had Rob's classes changed.

Like many parents, Pat and Jim had conferences with the teachers. They arranged for Rob to bring home progress reports every week. Rob brought the report home for two weeks. After that, he always had an excuse for not having it.

30 | Rob didn't do his chores around the house. He stayed out late. It seemed to Pat that she was always nagging him about something. Both his parents were unhappy when Rob didn't want to go places with the family. He talked back all the time, especially to his mother. He was fighting more with his sister, Lisa, too. When he wasn't fighting, Rob shut himself in his room and listened to his stereo. Pat was confused and hurt by his behavior. Jim was angry.

Harmful Involvement

As Rob got more into his drug use, Pat and Jim tried to cover even more for him. Jim decided to make sure that Rob got to school. Every morning, he woke up Rob and dropped him off at school on the way to work. Rob walked in the front door of the school and out the back.

When his parents discovered that Rob was stealing from them, they asked him about it. He lied, of course. He told them they were terrible parents because they didn't trust him. Pat and Jim felt guilty.

When the arguments started to get worse, Rob's parents tried all kinds of punishments. None worked. If they

Drinking and listening to the stereo can become a teenager's way of life—even TV can seem too much trouble.

Wondering becomes certainty when a teenager finds drugs in her brother's jeans.

grounded him, Rob sneaked out the window after everyone had gone to bed.

Pat knew that Rob smoked marijuana. She found it in the pockets of his pants and shirts when she washed his clothes. She didn't tell Jim about it. She didn't ask Rob about it. She was afraid he might be doing other drugs, too. She didn't want to know. It was too frightening to think about.

Because they were so involved with Rob, his parents paid little attention to their other child. They snapped at Lisa. Their shouting frightened her. These were not the parents Lisa knew. Her parents were fighting with each other over Rob. The family was coming apart.

When the call came from the police that Rob had been arrested, Pat didn't know what to do. She told Jim that she thought Rob was using drugs.

When they saw Rob at the juvenile center, Jim got angry. He accused Rob of using drugs and said he had to stop. Rob shouted that he would do what he wanted. Rob was given a date to appear in court and was sent home with his parents.

Whether or not the family goes into Stage 4 depends on what they do now.

34 Will they reach out for help for Rob and for themselves? Help is as close as the telephone. Who will make the move? If no one does, their disease of codependence will get worse along with Rob's disease of addiction.

Dependence

Many parents are in a similar position—they don't want their teen to go to jail. They hire lawyers and do all they can to keep the user out of jail. Then they expect him to shape up and be grateful. But the behavior just gets worse.

Parents soon give up trying to get their drug-using teens to go to school. The fights get worse. Name-calling, cursing, and shouting get worse. Anger is so intense that physical abuse is common.

When the fighting gets bad, users often leave. They take off for days and weeks. The family is relieved, but the parents worry about their child's safety.

Parents of children in Stage 4 feel hopeless and helpless. They feel that they have failed as parents and as people. Feelings of hatred for the user make them feel guilty. The schools and the courts tell them to do "something" about their chil-

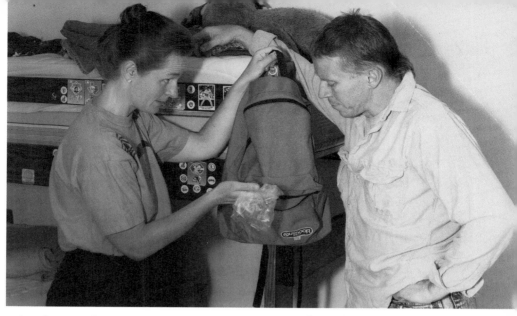

A family struggling with a drug user falls into verbal and physical violence.

dren. But no one tells them *how* to do "something" or *what* that something is.

It is not unusual for parents to throw teen addicts out of the house. The parents give up on them. Parents see that the whole family is suffering. They feel guilty because the other children have been hurt. They feel lost and helpless. Parents need support from people who understand. There are people in your community who can help.

Helping the Family

There are many options for a teen addict and for families of addicts. Look for treatment centers advertised on television and the radio. County agencies that help teens involved with drugs and their families

36 | can be found in the phone book. There are a great deal of support organizations available for parents; you can find some of their addresses at the back of this book.

CHAPTER 5

What's the Matter with Me?

"*No matter what I do, Sal doesn't appreciate it," César thought. "I try to help him, and he treats me like dirt. Sometimes I hate him. I don't know what to do anymore."*

César is confused and unhappy. Whatever he does or says makes no difference. He feels helpless.

César is caught in his brother's disease. Siblings (brothers and sisters) of addicts go through four stages in their codependence, just as their siblings go through four stages of their addiction.

Experimenting and Regular Use
Siblings of users often know when the drug use begins. A brother may come

Keeping the secret of a sibling's drug abuse makes for a lonely life.

home and brag about what a good time he had. When Sal first talked about drinking beer and getting high, César got a kind of thrill out of it. He was interested in knowing what it felt like to be high on marijuana. He didn't think much about Sal's drinking and using until his trouble at school started.

Although César and Sal got along pretty well, they had always had arguments. When the drug use started, the reasons for fighting changed. Sal was so touchy that he got mad over everything. He started picking on their younger brother Paulo too. That made Paulo try harder to please him.

When Sal needed to get into the house at night, Paulo let him in. César covered for Sal, too. The more they covered for Sal, the worse his behavior became. By covering for Sal, they were enablers. As enablers, they saved Sal from the bad things that would have happened if his behavior were found out. They helped him to continue using and to progress to Stage 3.

Harmful Involvement

As Sal's drug use got worse, César became more upset by Sal's behavior. He told Sal he was messing up. César wanted

40 Sal to shape up. Sal told him to mind his own business.

César could not tell his parents what was going on. He had covered for Sal for so long that he couldn't tell on him now. His parents were hurting too much already. Besides, César was afraid of what Sal might do if he told.

Poor Paulo was really in a bad position. He knew almost all of Sal's secrets. When Sal took off for days, he got Paulo to bring him food and clothes. Paulo knew that Sal was doing something bad. He wanted his parents to stop Sal, but he couldn't tell them what Sal was doing. Confused and helpless, he kept covering for Sal.

César and Paulo wanted their parents to do something about Sal. Yelling and fighting went nowhere. Sal just got worse. Their parents didn't act like the same people anymore. Nobody talked to anybody at home.

Paulo was confused and hated all the fighting. He wanted his parents to notice him, but they didn't. He tried being bad like Sal to get their attention. His mother kept saying, "What's the matter with you? You know better than that." Paulo couldn't be bad enough to make his

parents notice. Besides, he felt so guilty,
he went back to being good.

Although he didn't know what to do,
César was very worried. When Sal was
coming off drugs and needed more, he
was dangerous. César had to do something. Would that "something" help César
stop Sal's disease from getting worse, or
would it be a step into Stage 4?

Dependence

As parents give up on the user, so do the
brothers and sisters. Those who are older
leave home. They go away to school or
move out on their own as soon as possi-
ble. Younger siblings may stay at friends'
homes. Getting away is the most common
behavior in Stage 4.

If your mother is a single mother, you
may feel that your job is to protect her.
Younger brothers and sisters may look to
you for protection. You want to leave,
yet you feel tied to the family by this
huge responsibility. You are angry
because of the responsibility put on you.
But you feel guilty for wanting to get
away. You are caught in the trap of
codependence.

By the time you reach Stage 4, everyone feels powerless and lost. No one

Sometimes running away seems like the only answer for a teenager in a family fighting over a sibling's drug abuse.

wants to be part of the family. You want someone to wave a magic wand, make your brother or sister well, and make all the hurt disappear.

Magic does not happen, but recovery does. There are things you can do to help your brother or sister. You can be the one to take the first step toward stopping the progression of the disease in your family.

CHAPTER 6

How You Can Help

T aking a deep breath, Lynn reached for the phone book. I can't take any more, she thought. Somebody in this family has to do something about Sonya. Lynn looked up Drug Abuse in the Yellow Pages. She picked up the phone, dialed the first three numbers and put the phone down. She looked at the phone for a long time and then picked it up again. Her heart was pounding as she dialed the number and waited for someone to answer. "I want to help my sister. She does drugs. What can I do?"

Ask for Help
When you don't know what to do, ask for help. You can't handle the problem alone.

The teenager with a drug-addicted sibling needs someone to talk to most of all.

There are people who can help your family. A simple phone call can start the process. Lynn looked under Drug Abuse in the Yellow Pages. This is a good place to start.

Don't Cover-up

Maybe you've been covering for your brother or sister. You are making it easier for them to use drugs. Here are behaviors to watch out for. If you are doing any of them, STOP. You are *not* helping anyone in the family.

- Letting them in when doors are locked
- Covering for them when they break rules

46

- Lending them money
- Not telling when they steal from the family
- Taking them food and clothing when they run away
- Always fighting with them
- Letting them have their way to avoid making them angry
- Siding with them against your parents
- Doing their schoolwork
- Pretending everything is fine

What Will Help?

It is time to talk about all the secrets. Your parents need to know what is going on. If you cannot talk to your parents, talk to an adult you trust. That person can help you talk to your parents. If your school has a drug abuse counselor, talk to him or her. Working with families is an important part of that counselor's job.

Lynn looked for help from a treatment center. That is a good place to learn about chemical dependence. Treatment centers often have classes for families of drug users. The counselors explain how to get someone like Sonya to go for help. Someone there can help you talk to your parents.

Your parents need support, too. TOUGHLOVE Parent Support Groups help parents deal with their troubled teens. Parents in the TOUGHLOVE group have experience dealing with the behavior of drug users. They know what parents must do to get help for their teens.

Your other brothers and sisters need to know about the disease of chemical dependence, too. They need to understand that the drug user in your family is very ill. They need to know that the whole family has this illness. Most of all, they need someone to listen to their feelings and their fears. You can support them when they talk to your parents.

Not all families are willing to get help. Your parents may not want to hear what you have to say. The rest of the family may not understand what you want to do. Even if the disease is not stopped for the rest of your family, you can get help for yourself.

CHAPTER 7

Helping Yourself

Marcus looked around the group. He knew almost everybody there. Some were brothers and sisters of his brother's druggie friends. Others had fathers or mothers who were alcoholics or drug users. They all knew about Keith. They told Marcus not to feel guilty about his brother—that he had no reason to be embarrassed. He almost hadn't come, but now he planned to come back next week. He didn't feel alone anymore.

Find Support

You can't deal with a drug-using sibling by yourself. You need support. Marcus's school has a Student Assistance Program

A teenager with an addicted sibling needs to get out and make a life for herself.

50 and a special counselor to hold group meetings for students affected by another's drug use. Check at your school about a support group for yourself.

Talk to an adult you trust—a teacher, a coach, or a school counselor. The parent of a friend is often easier to talk to than your own parents. A relative who really listens to you can help. Don't try to make it on your own or with just your peers. Find an adult who can help you.

It's Not Your Fault

Sometimes Marcus and Keith had terrible fights. Like many brothers and sisters of drug users, Marcus felt guilty and thought the fights made Keith use drugs more.

The group told Mike about the 3 Cs. You didn't CAUSE the drug use. You can't CONTROL it, and you can't CURE it. Nothing you do causes anyone to drink or use. If you've been blaming your parents or drug-using friends, it's not their fault either. Remember the 3 Cs. No one is to blame.

Don't Hide

It's tough when you go to the same school as your drug-using brother or sister. You don't want people to think you're like him or her. Don't let the drug user keep you from doing what you want to do. Take part in activities you like. You need to have a life outside of home. It's important to have friends who are cheerful, supportive, and involved in positive activities. Don't worry. You'll be accepted for who you are.

Don't Take It Personally

The disease of addiction causes users to take what they want. Try not to take it personally if they yell at you or steal from you. It doesn't do any good to get mad at them. Get mad at the disease.

Stay Away from Drugs and Alcohol

Living with a drug-using brother or sister puts you at high risk for becoming chemically dependent. Drinking or drug abusing teens think it's fun to get brothers and sisters loaded. They tell you how great it is and are a handy source of drugs for you. They want a buddy at home. Don't fall into the trap.

Safety First

Drug users can get violent quickly and without warning. If your brother or sister is violent, don't take any chances. Leave,

52 | if you can and go somewhere safe. If you're embarrassed to go to a neighbor's house, go anyway. Go to a friend. Get to a safe place. If you're afraid you'll be hurt, call 911. If you're afraid your parents will be upset if you call the police, call 911 anyway. Your safety is the most important thing.

Be Your Own Best Friend

You can find support outside your home, but your most important support is found within yourself. You need to be good to yourself.

Only you can give yourself back the self-esteem this disease robs from you. You can't handle this problem alone. You don't need to. Ask for help. You *may* lead your family to recovery. Even if your family won't listen, you can find *your* way to recovery. Get help. *You* are worth it.

FACT SHEET

- In a 1996 survey of high school seniors:

  40.8 percent used an illegal drug in the last year;

  26.5 percent used an illegal drug in the last thirty days;

  37.9 percent used marijuana in the last year.

- Alcohol is the drug most used by teens today.

- Girls today are fifteen times more likely than their mothers to begin using illegal drugs by age fifteen.

- The trading of sex for drugs or for money to buy drugs is a major cause of the spread of HIV and AIDS.

54

- Of high school students who
  reported carrying a gun to school:
      83.6 percent drank liquor;
      78.0 percent smoked marijuana;
      36.5 percent used cocaine.
- Of high school students who reported taking part in gang activities:
      78.6 percent drank liquor;
      69.3 percent smoked marijuana;
      21.6 percent used cocaine.
- 85.5 percent of sixth graders thought
  marijuana was "very harmful" to
  their health. Only 43.6 percent of
  twelfth graders thought the same.
- Between 1988 and 1996, marijuana
  use by twelfth graders increased 147
  percent.
- Someone is injured in an alcohol-
  related crash every minute and a half.
- In 1990, 30.8 percent of sixteen- to
  twenty-year-old drivers killed in car
  crashes were drunk.
- Fifteen- to twenty-year-olds represent
  8 percent of drivers and have 17
  percent of alcohol-related fatal
  crashes.
- Almost half of all traffic deaths are
  alcohol-related.
- Someone is killed by a drunk driver
  every twenty-four minutes.

- More than 40 percent of all deaths
for fifteen- to twenty-year-olds were
from car accidents. Almost 50 percent were alcohol related.
- More than 30 percent of fifteen- to
twenty-year-olds killed in car accidents were drunk.
- One in 120 males who are fifteen
years old will die in a car accident
before his twenty-fifth birthday.
- 60 percent of convicted drunk
drivers said they drank beer only.
- From 1979 to 1990, alcohol-related
traffic accidents decreased 12 percent
for males and increased 21 percent
for females.

Glossary
Explaining New Words

acid   Street name for the hallucinogen LSD.

addiction   Being hooked on a drug so much that the user continues to take it no matter what happens to himself or herself or others.

Al-Anon   A community group of people who are affected by someone else's alcohol (and other drug) use. They meet and share feelings and help one another deal with problems.

Alateen   A community group of young people who are affected by someone else's alcohol (and other drug) use. They meet to share feelings and help one another deal with problems.

Alcoholics Anonymous (AA)   A community group of chemically dependent people who meet to share feelings and help one another stay well and not drink or use other drugs.

alcoholism An illness that causes people to become dependent on alcohol.

blackout Loss of memory of what happened while drinking or using other drugs.

chemical dependence Craving a drug so much that it causes people to keep taking the drug even when it is harmful and destroying their lives.

cocaine A powerful central nervous system stimulant taken from the leaves of the coca plant and made into a powder that is snorted, smoked, or injected.

Cocaine Anonymous (CA) A community group of cocaine addicts who meet to share feelings and help one another stay well and not use cocaine or other drugs.

codependent Someone affected by another person's chemical dependence.

compulsion Uncontrolled need to do something again and again.

denial Unwillingness to admit the truth; unwillingness to admit there is a problem with chemicals.

58 | **depression**   A feeling of deep sadness; feeling "down."

drug   A chemical substance that changes how the mind or body functions.

enable   To cover for the drug user so he or she does not experience the harmful effects of his or her behavior; to make it easier for someone to continue using drugs.

illegal   Against the law.

joint   Marijuana cigarette.

PCP   A strong hallucinogen.

peer   Someone your own age.

physiological dependence   Type of drug dependence that involves physical withdrawal symptoms when the drug is discontinued.

pot   Street name for marijuana.

prescription drugs   Medicines that must be ordered by a doctor and prepared by a pharmacist.

progression   Movement from one stage to another.

psychological dependence   Type of drug dependence that involves psychological needs, such as the need for approval.

speed   Street name for amphetamines; also called uppers, pep pills, bennies, exies, meth, crystal, crank.

stash Drug supply.

tolerance Needing more of the drug to
get the same effect.

withdrawal Cramps, fever, chills, shaking, and upset stomach that happens
when drug use is stopped; the feeling
of anxiety, fear, and confusion that
happens when the user stops taking
drugs.

Where to Go for Help

Telephone Book

Yellow Pages

• Alcoholism, Drug Abuse, Counselors

White Pages

• Alcoholics Anonymous, Al-Anon, Narcotics Anonymous, National Council of Alcoholism, Alcoholism, Counseling, Drug Abuse Services, Cocaine Anonymous, Alateen (Call Al-Anon and ask about Alateen), Government Listings
• Alcoholism Treatment, Drug Abuse, County Health Services

Write or Call

Al-Anon/Alateen Family Groups
1600 Corporate Landing Parkway
Virginia Beach, VA 23454
(800) 356-9996
(757) 563-1600
Web site: http://www.alanon.alateen.org

National Association for Children of Alcoholics
11426 Rockville Pike, Suite 100
Rockville, MD 20852
(888) 554-2627
(301) 468-0985
Web site: http://www.health.org/NACoA

National Clearinghouse for Alcohol and Drug
    Information
P.O. Box 2345
Rockville, MD 20652
(301) 468-2600
Web site: http://www.health.org
Email address: info@ prevline.health.org

National Council on Alcoholism and Drug Dependence | *61*
12 West 21st Street
New York, NY 10010
(800) 622-2255
(212) 206-6770
Web site: http://www.ncadd.org
Email address: national@ NCADD.org

TOUGHLOVE International
P.O. Box 1069
Doylestown, PA 18901
(800) 333-1069
Web site: http://ourworld. compuserve.com.80/
    homepages/ TOUGHLOVE

CANADA

Alcoholics Anonymous:
202 Intergroup Office
234 Ellington Avenue E.
Toronto, ON M4P1K5
(416) 487-5591
Manitoba Central Office
505-365 Hargrave St.
Winnipeg, Manitoba R3B2K3
(204) 942-0126

Hot lines

1-800-COCAINE Answers any questions about
    cocaine.
1-800-67-PRIDE For information about alcohol and
    drugs.

Places That Have Support Groups

- Your city's National Council on Alcoholism
- County Mental Health Services
- County Juvenile Services
- Your school counseling office
- Your school nurse
- Teen clinic

For Further Reading

Ball, Jacqueline A. *Everything You Need to Know about Drug Abuse.* New York: The Rosen Publishing Group, 1992.

Hull-Mast, Nancy, and Diane Purcell. *Sibs: The Forgotten Family Members.* Park Ridge, Ill: Parkside Publishing, 1989.

Myers, Arthur. *Drugs and Emotions.* New York: The Rosen Publishing Group, 1996.

Challenging Reading

Edwards, Gabrielle I. *Coping with Drug Abuse.* Rev. ed. New York: The Rosen Publishing Group, 1990.

Porterfield, Kay Marie. *Coping with Codependency.* New York: The Rosen Publishing Group, 1997.

Scott, Sharon. *How to Say No and Keep Your Friends.* Amherst, Mass.: Human Resource Development Press, Inc., 1986.

Index

About the Author

Rhoda McFarland has taught all grades from kindergarten through twelfth. She is a certified alcoholism and drug abuse counselor, having worked with troubled young people and their parents. She developed and implemented the first educational program in the California area for students making the transition from drug/alcohol treatment programs back into the regular school system.

Photo Credits

Cover photo: Chuck Peterson
Photos on pages 2, 6, 12, 17, 21, 24, 30, 32, 39; Michael F. O'Brien; pages 29, 35, 42, 51: Stuart Rabinowitz; page 47: Chris Volpe